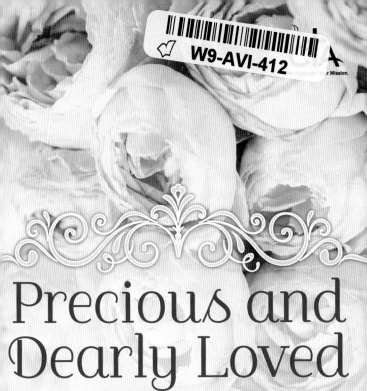

Precious and Dearly Loved

Devotions for Women

Gail Marsh

The vision of CTA is to see Christians highly effective in their ministry so that Christ's Kingdom is strengthened and expanded.

Precious and Dearly Loved

Gail Marsh

Copyright © 2018 CTA, Inc.
1625 Larkin Williams Rd.
Fenton, MO 63026
www.CTAinc.com

Unless otherwise indicated, Scripture quotations are from the ESV® Bible (The Holy Bible, English Standard Version®), copyright © 2001 by Crossway, a publishing ministry of Good News Publishers. Used by permission. All rights reserved.

Scripture quotations marked NLT are from the Holy Bible, New Living Translation copyright © 1996, 2004, 2007, 2013, 2015 by Tyndale House Foundation. Used by permission of Tyndale House Publishers Inc., Carol Stream, Illinois 60188. All rights reserved.

ISBN 978-1-943216-56-7
PRINTED IN THAILAND

Positively Precious!

I have loved you with an everlasting love.
Jeremiah 31:3

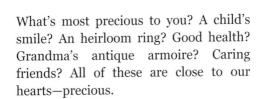

What's most precious to you? A child's smile? An heirloom ring? Good health? Grandma's antique armoire? Caring friends? All of these are close to our hearts—precious.

But consider this. You (yes, you!) are precious to your heavenly Father! It's true! You are so precious that he sacrificed his very own, beloved and precious Son so you could belong to his forever family!

During the coming week, we'll take a closer look at your heavenly Father's love. He does love you! Really. Loves. You. Words from Scripture—your Father's very own words—will comfort and encourage you as you see the truth: You are positively precious to the Lord.

Preciously Loved

The God of love and peace will be with you.

2 Corinthians 13:11

It was simple in design. Five-inch yarn squares joined together to make a soft coverlet. My mother wove each square on a small loom that fit in her hands. Up and over. Down and through. Line by line, she added yarn until the little loom was filled. Then, after carefully removing the finished square, Mom began again.

When all of the yarn squares were completed, Mom placed them on the living room floor, arranging them in the way she thought looked best. Finally, she used variegated yarn to join the squares to make a small coverlet.

She called it her afghan, and it seems as if someone in the family used it every day! If we were feeling sick, mom covered us with the afghan until we recovered. Several family members could fit under the afghan's warm embrace while watching television. It even made a pretty good imaginary "tent" when flung over a couple of dining room chairs.

Mom is in heaven now, and I'm not sure what happened to her afghan. I remember it, though, and how wonderful it felt to be wrapped up in it on a cold winter's day. Just thinking about the simply woven cover reminds me of mom's love, creativity, and care.

I'm reminded of the afghan, too, when I read today's Scripture verse. Mom's afghan serves as a simplified picture of God's love and peace—for me, and for you! First, God's love is intentional. He knows us intimately and because he knows us, he knows what we need. Because of our sin, we desperately need to be forgiven, to be reconciled with a holy God. And that's where love comes in.

Love drove Jesus to his cross, and victoriously up from the grave. Because of all Jesus did, our Father's love now surrounds us with healing, comfort, and peace. His love for us, his precious daughters, is unfailing. Constant. Reliable. Because God is love, his love for us never fails or fades. He continually loves us and, through Jesus, extends grace to us in every circumstance.

 PRAYER STARTER: Dear Father, help me recognize your love and draw peaceful comfort from it as I live for you today. Enable me to share that love with others, especially when . . .

Adopted and Precious

God decided in advance to adopt us into his own family by bringing us to himself through Jesus Christ. This is what he wanted to do, and it gave him great pleasure.

Ephesians 1:5 NLT

Little bundle of joy. That's what her adoptive family called her. They'd waited years to hold her in their arms. The pain of past miscarriages and failed fertility treatments faded from memory as they watched her sleep. Breathe in. So precious! Breathe out. You're loved! Breathe in. What joy! Breathe out. You're ours!

Adoption takes determination and planning, but most of all adoption takes love—the gritty kind of love that doesn't give up. It's a tenacious love that keeps moving forward, no matter the cost.

God, our heavenly Father, approached our own adoption into his family with similar no-holds-barred determination and gritty, genuine love! Ephesians 1:5

details our Father's plan, and it hints at how much our adoption would eventually cost him. It's astounding, really! Why would God want to adopt us? We have nothing to offer a holy God. We are, by our very nature, self-centered and rebellious—not exactly a glowing recommendation!

Yet, our Father's determination (and yes, love) urged him to pursue our adoption. Even though it came at a very high price:

Christ has rescued us from the curse pronounced by the law. When he was hung on the cross, he took upon himself the curse for our wrongdoing. For it is written in the Scriptures, "Cursed is everyone who is hung on a tree."

Galatians 3:13 NLT

Was our adoption worth it? Jesus, our brother, thinks so. It's what our adoptive Father wanted to do. In fact, bringing us into his forever family gave God our Father great pleasure! Just imagine—when we were made part of that family, God smiled! He smiled over us with great joy.

Even now, he watches over us. Breathe in. "You're so precious to me!" Breathe out. "I love you!" Breathe in. "I'm so happy!" God says, "You're mine!"

PRAYER STARTER: Oh, Father, how can I thank you for making me part of your very own family? I'm humbled and so grateful for your love! Help me think, speak, and act as your dearly loved and redeemed daughter even when . . .

Most Precious

You yourselves have seen what I did to the Egyptians, and how I bore you on eagles' wings and brought you to myself. Now therefore, if you will indeed obey my voice and keep my covenant, you shall be my treasured possession among all peoples, for all the earth is mine.

Exodus 19:4–5

For several years I collected items from the Precious Moments collection. I was drawn to the teardrop-eyed children featured as figurines, Christmas tree ornaments, and framed artwork. Soon family members and friends knew about my collection and gladly contributed to it on birthdays and other special events. I treasured my collection, and so I kept the fragile figurines safely inside a glass-doored hutch.

Then, at Christmastime, one of my kindergarten students presented me with a gift. I wondered if this child-decorated gift bag bore another Precious Moments item to add to my collection. I carefully unwrapped it and held it up. "It's not a real Precious Moment, but it's still precious!" the little giver quickly shouted.

I examined the simple, dollar-store ceramic nativity and smiled. "Out of the mouths of babes," I thought. Aloud, I said, "I'll certainly add it to my collection. I think it's precious, too."

The nativity gift still sits next to the genuine Precious Moments figurines in the hutch. Out of all the items in my collection, I prize it most of all. It serves as a reminder to me that value, as well as beauty, is in the eye of the beholder. When God looks at me, his dearly redeemed child, he sees me not as I really am, but who he has made me through Jesus. I am his treasured possession! And so are you!

Read today's Scripture verse one more time. God is reminding his Old Testament people (along with you and me) how he has demonstrated love and care for his children in the past. Nothing could stop our God! Not slavery. Not Pharaoh's army. Not a churning Red Sea. Not a rebellious past. Not *(name your own troubling challenge)*! None of it can change the fact that we are God's treasured possession. Now and forever!

 PRAYER STARTER: Today, Lord, I want to see myself as you see me: loved, forgiven, treasured, and precious in your sight. Help me . . .

Precious Rags

We have all become like one who is unclean,
and all our righteous deeds are like a polluted
garment. We all fade like a leaf, and our iniquities,
like the wind, take us away.

Isaiah 64:6

An oxymoron is a unique figure of speech where two opposite ideas come together. Jumbo shrimp. Bitter sweet. Civil war. False positive.

That last one got my attention a few years ago. Shortly after a routine mammogram the doctor's office called to say I'd need a follow-up. Turns out, there was nothing wrong. Yearly tests afterward were negative. The original positive turned out to be a "false positive."

But because of that one false positive, I now sometimes hear a "what if" whispering in the back of my mind. When I hear it, I need to remind myself: false positives happen. They are false. Positively false.

Sometimes I struggle with "false positive" faith, too. I'm precious to God? Really? Many days my thoughts and actions are anything but precious! I snipe at my family. I do only the bare minimum at work. I even rail against God: "Why can't we ever have enough money to pay all the bills?" Precious? Me? Not at all!

When my sinful attitude, words, and actions are set beside my holy God, the contrast makes me want to hide in embarrassment and fear. Even on a good day, the Lord looks past my outward attempts all the way into my heart. There, he clearly sees my self-serving motivations. My good deeds are no more than dirty rags!

But when I think that, I need to remind myself of the truth:

You were his enemies, separated from him by your evil thoughts and actions. Yet now he has reconciled you to himself through the death of Christ in his physical body. As a result, he has brought you into his own presence, and you are holy and blameless as you stand before him without a single fault.

Colossians 1:21–22 NLT

The filthy rags are gone. They've been washed clean! Pure! In fact, they've been transformed into a robe of righteousness! It's true! Positively true!

PRAYER STARTER: Remind me, gracious Father, that because of Jesus, I can be sure—positively certain—that I belong to you, today and always! Thank you for . . .

Love's Cornerstone

I am laying in Zion a stone, a cornerstone chosen and precious, and whoever believes in him will not be put to shame.

1 Peter 2:6

"Only the best is good enough." You may not recognize this motto, but you undoubtedly know the product. It originated in Denmark in the 1930s and continues to be one of the most popular products sold throughout the world today. With 19 billion pieces manufactured annually, this brand is practically synonymous with childhood imagination and play: LEGO bricks!

The word *cornerstone* was as familiar to people in biblical times as the LEGO brand is to us today. Ancient builders chose cornerstones with great care. And for good reason! The weight of the building in large part rested upon this first-laid stone. Every brick mortared into position was carefully aligned with the cornerstone so that the walls would remain level, plumb, and strong. Only the very best of stones qualified to be used as cornerstones.

With all of this in mind, reread 1 Peter 2:6. Do you recognize in these words God's blueprint for salvation? "Only the best is good enough" for your heavenly Father's kingdom-building design. God's wonderful plan of salvation rests upon Jesus, the perfect Cornerstone.

With love as his sole motivation, your Savior became a true human being. He accepted the limitations of a physical body. Through human eyes he saw the hopelessness of sinful humankind. Jesus chose suffering, humiliation, pain, and cruel death to rescue you. Yes, you! Why? Because you are precious to God. How precious? So precious that he gave up his only beloved Son. For you!

Here's how your heavenly Father puts it:

I have loved you, my people, with an everlasting love. With unfailing love I have drawn you to myself.

Jeremiah 31:3 NLT

Did you catch that? Your heavenly Father is drawing you close. He is gathering you up in his arms and gently hugging you to his heart. He loves you! He has always loved you, and that's why he did it—why he sent his Son for you. You are precious. So very precious that the Father sent his very best. Jesus! For you!

 PRAYER STARTER: Thank you, Father! Thank you for sending nothing less than the best— your Son, Jesus—to be my Cornerstone and Savior. Teach me to trust you . . .

I have loved you with an everlasting love.

Jeremiah 31:3

Try reading this verse out loud. Add your own name to the verse, after the word *you*, to personalize these words from your Lord. Begin with a whisper. Read the verse again and again, raising your volume; then lower your volume back to a whisper.

These words from God are true! You are positively precious to your Lord. Ask him to help you positively believe it!

Lavishly Loved

I lavish unfailing love to a thousand generations.
Exodus 34:7 NLT

Lavish. Opulent. Extravagant. Overgenerous. When God pours out lavish love upon his people, it cascades into our lives like a midsummer downpour. We are deluged, soaked, immersed in divine love—inside and out.

With this picture in mind, ask yourself, "What does God really mean when he says, 'I lavish unfailing love . . .'?"

During the coming week, we'll explore God's lavish love and how he pours it out upon us. Ready? Let's get started!

Love's Lavish Lifestyle

I lavish unfailing love to a thousand generations.
I forgive iniquity, rebellion, and sin.

Exodus 34:7 NLT

"Champagne wishes and caviar dreams." That was the signature catchphrase of Robin Leach, host of the television show *Lifestyles of the Rich and Famous*. The show aired for more than a decade, from the mid-eighties to mid-nineties. Viewers saw the opulent lives of actors, athletes, and business moguls. Still today, magazines, tabloids, and TV shows help us peek into the lives of the rich and famous.

So why the fascination? Opinions differ, but some say that escaping into the carefree world of the very wealthy—even for just 30 minutes—somehow helps us cope with our own lives. After all, the wealthy never struggle with their household budgets, a leaky roof, or bad hair days. (Do they?) The "good life" beckons, and viewers respond.

Today's verse from Scripture hints at something better than the "good life" enjoyed by celebrities. It describes, in fact, a great life! A life upon which God lavishes his magnificent love! Because we belong to the triune God, we need not fret and stew about household budgets or bad-hair days either! Our peace has nothing to do with our net worth; it has everything to do with our almighty Lord.

Jesus himself reassures us:

Do not be anxious about your life, what you will eat or what you will drink, nor about your body, what you will put on. Is not life more than food, and the body more than clothing? Look at the birds of the air: they neither sow nor reap nor gather into barns, and yet your heavenly Father feeds them. Are you not of more value than they?

Matthew 6:25–26

Of course, you're more valuable! You were so valuable that Jesus Christ, God's only Son, died in your place! His sacrifice on the cross and resurrection from the dead has made you, through faith, a daughter of the King! Heaven awaits you!

And until then, your life here on earth is flooded with God's love, as he provides the very best for you—no matter what! You have to admit that's much, much better than dreaming of caviar!

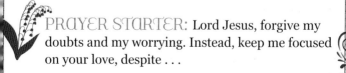

PRAYER STARTER: Lord Jesus, forgive my doubts and my worrying. Instead, keep me focused on your love, despite . . .

Pray

In him you also, when you heard the word of truth, the gospel of your salvation, and believed in him, were sealed with the promised Holy Spirit.

Ephesians 1:13

Many historians place St. Augustine on the short list of the most important Christian leaders of all time. But maybe you don't know much about Augustine's mother, Monica. Monica's husband was a pagan who initially rejected Christianity, but Monica was a Christian woman who loved her family and was concerned for their salvation. She taught her boys about the Lord from little on, and she prayed.

Monica prayed especially for Augustine. Early on, she recognized his great intelligence and his natural leadership skills. Monica encouraged Augustine in his education, supported his efforts, and continued to intercede for him before the throne of God.

In his teens, Augustine scornfully rejected the faith to pursue pagan philosophies. Monica wept but continued to pray. Immersing himself in the pursuit of self-gratification and immorality, Augustine lived with a woman who was not his wife and fathered a son. Still, Monica prayed. And prayed. For thirty years, Augustine's mother cried out to God for her son's salvation. And then, it happened. A mother's prayers were answered. Tears of despair and frustration became tears of joy.

Monica's story may strike close to home for you. Almost everyone has shed a tear over a child or grandchild or niece or parent who has walked away from God. We wonder if our loved ones will ever return to the truths they learned in their youth. And what about our dear nephews, uncles, aunts, and friends who have rejected the Lord? What will happen to them? What can I do—as their mom, friend, daughter?

The answer seems too simplistic to be real, but here it is: pray. That's what God wants us to do. Pray to your heavenly Father for the right words to say and the right time to say them. Your Savior loves your loved ones! He loves them even more than you do! He will not coerce anyone into the kingdom, but he does want to love them into his arms. God hears your prayers. Keep praying!

PRAYER STARTER: Lord Jesus, you love *[names]* even more than I do. Teach me how to pray and remind me to keep praying . . .

Lavish Dimensions
of God's Love

And to know the love of Christ that surpasses knowledge.

Ephesians 3:19

"I just can't see it," Shawna murmured as she studied the blueprints. "I mean, I see the lines, but I need a model of the house in order to tell everything's just right." Building the home of her dreams, Shawna wanted everything to be perfect. The two-dimensional rendering didn't quite do it for Shawna. So the architect prepared a model. Smiling at the three-dimensional prototype, Shawna grinned, "I love it! This house will be perfect!"

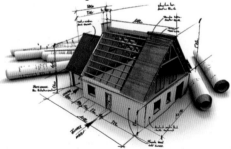

The more dimensions, the better. How many dimensions can you count in the words around today's Bible verse? Through the apostle Paul, God describes his lavish love in four dimensions! Four! To get the full picture, read this section of Scripture:

I bow my knees before the Father, from whom every family in heaven and on earth is named, that according to the riches of his glory he may grant you to be strengthened with power through his Spirit in your inner being, so that Christ may dwell in your hearts through faith—that you, being rooted and grounded in love, may have strength to comprehend with all the saints what is the breadth and length and height and depth, and to know the love of Christ that surpasses knowledge, that you may be filled with all the fullness of God.

Ephesians 3:14–19

God's lavish love is mind-blowing! How can we begin to wrap our brain around the width, length, height, and depth of God's love for us? It's impossible! The wonder of it all sends Paul to his knees!

We won't completely grasp our Father's lavish love until we reach heaven. Even then, it will take an eternity to explore its every facet. In the meantime, Christ makes himself at home, right in our hearts. The Holy Spirit continues his work in us, drawing upon resources that have no limits.

Picture it! Roots of faith pressing more deeply into the soil of God's love. The life of faith sprouting up and growing into a richer and richer understanding of that love—love poured out. A veritable deluge of love. Lavish love. For you and me. Forever!

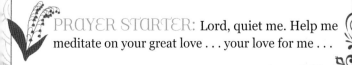

PRAYER STARTER: Lord, quiet me. Help me meditate on your great love . . . your love for me . . .

Stored Goodness

How great is the goodness you have stored up for those who fear you. You lavish it on those who come to you for protection, blessing them before the watching world.

Psalm 31:19 NLT

As you grew up, did you have a hope chest? In recent decades, this once-common custom has become almost obsolete—falling out of tradition since the mid-'70s. But in earlier centuries, the hope chest was seen as a way for a woman to contribute to her future household.

Traditionally, the hope chest was made of wood, often cedar, and was filled, little by little, with household linens, kitchenware, bedding, and clothing. These items were collected over the course of several years, with the idea that one day a young woman would use her "household trousseau" to set up her first home away from home, whether with her husband or on her own. In many cases, items inside the hope chest included handmade gifts from relatives, jewelry, quilts, and heirlooms passed down from one generation to the next.

There's something happily optimistic about a hope chest. Imagine peeking inside one now. Imagine breathing in the pungent cedar smell. Catch a glimpse of your own "blessing trousseau" as you reread today's Bible verse.

For all eternity, your lavishly loving Lord has been storing up goodness—for you. This goodness is so much better than hand-embroidered pillowcases or antique jewelry. It far outweighs the value of any treasured family heirloom. What is this "great goodness"?

But for me it is good to be near God; I have made the Lord GOD my refuge, that I may tell of all your works.

Psalm 73:28

Real blessing, true goodness, is to be near God. Contrary to popular belief, God's greatest gifts to his people are not health or wealth, notoriety or power. Nearness to our heavenly Father is the ultimate good, the ultimate blessing.

Our good and gracious heavenly Father loved us so lavishly that he made nearness to him possible—through his Son. Through the cross and empty tomb of Jesus, God made it possible to pour out his lavish love on us. Now, God holds you close to his heart. Always.

PRAYER STARTER: Lord Jesus, hold me close to yourself today. Remind me that nearness to you is the best blessing of all . . .

A Lavish Feast

On this mountain the LORD of hosts will make for all peoples a feast of rich food, a feast of well-aged wine, of rich food full of marrow, of aged wine well refined. And he will swallow up on this mountain the covering that is cast over all peoples, the veil that is spread over all nations.

Isaiah 25:6–7

What's the best meal you've ever eaten? Was it a Thanksgiving feast with your extended family? Or perhaps your favorite meal of all time was the big potluck feast hosted by your church. Or could it have been an all-you-can-eat buffet at your favorite restaurant? Or a very special meal carefully prepared by your own hands?

What's the best meal you've ever eaten? As you think about your answer, do you recall the beautiful way in which the food was presented? Does your mouth water as you remember the aroma wafting from the oven, the food's fantastic flavors?

What country's cuisine do you like best? Asian? Mexican? Peruvian? The list seems endless because today's food culture includes so many different ethnicities. You've probably sampled recipes originating from countries all around the world. Perhaps you've even tried your hand at cooking some ethnic delicacies on your own.

Food. People everywhere understand its importance and crave their favorite flavors. Almost every celebration we can imagine is connected with food of some kind, whether a simple snack or an elaborate feast.

Is it any wonder that our Lord chose to describe heaven in terms of a bountiful banquet? He wants us to catch a vision of what awaits those who belong to his forever family. That's not just you and me, but believers from every nation, every era since the beginning of time! The Bible goes on to say:

The Sovereign LORD will wipe away all tears. He will remove forever all insults and mockery against his land and people. The LORD has spoken! In that day the people will proclaim, "This is our God! We trusted in him, and he saved us! This is the LORD, in whom we trusted. Let us rejoice in the salvation he brings!"

Isaiah 25:8–9 NLT

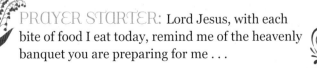

PRAYER STARTER: Lord Jesus, with each bite of food I eat today, remind me of the heavenly banquet you are preparing for me . . .

You prepare a table before me in the presence of my enemies; you anoint my head with oil; my cup overflows.

Psalm 23:5

On another sheet of paper, begin a list of blessings your heavenly Father has, in love, lavished upon you. Think of tangible blessings and of intangible ones, as well. Tuck the list inside your Bible and add to it daily. Let your list of blessings become an ongoing psalm of thanks and praise to your lavishly loving Lord.

Perfectly Protected

The LORD of Heaven's Armies sent me against the nations who plundered you. For he said, "Anyone who harms you harms my most precious possession."

Zechariah 2:8 NLT

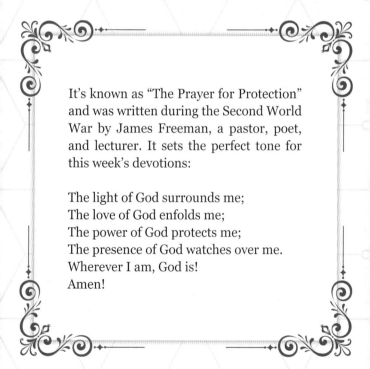

It's known as "The Prayer for Protection" and was written during the Second World War by James Freeman, a pastor, poet, and lecturer. It sets the perfect tone for this week's devotions:

The light of God surrounds me;
The love of God enfolds me;
The power of God protects me;
The presence of God watches over me.
Wherever I am, God is!
Amen!

Perfect Light

The LORD came from Mount Sinai and dawned upon us from Mount Seir; he shone forth from Mount Paran and came from Meribah-kadesh with flaming fire at his right hand. Indeed, he loves his people; all his holy ones are in his hands.

Deuteronomy 33:2–3 NLT

Venice, Italy, is the home of the magnificent *Palazzo Ducale*. This Gothic-style palace functions as a center for cultural events in Venice. It also houses many works of art. One particular painting found there has four panels. Entitled *Visions of the Hereafter*, it was painted by the fifteenth-century artist Hieronymus Bosch.

One of the painting's four panels features a large tunnel. Light emanates from the end of this tunnel partially illuminating the lower half of the painting, which is shrouded in darkness. In this darkness, angels escort people up and into the tunnel. The artist titled this panel of his painting "Ascent of the Blessed."

I wonder whether the expression "the light at the end of the tunnel" came from Bosch's painting. Much more important, though, is this question: "Does the painting align with what God says in his Word?" To answer that, reread Deuteronomy 33:2–3. Do you see any darkness?

Perhaps Bosch missed something, something critical to each adopted child of God. The Bible reminds us that our Lord has come to be with us, to be with us right now! He isn't waiting around at the end of some tunnel, his fingers crossed and hoping that one way or another we will successfully battle the evil around us and eventually make our way home to him.

Not at all! In his cross and resurrection Jesus already won that battle! His love and power surround us now and forever.

All of us experience dark days. Rejection stings. Illness brings pain. Loneliness aches. Disappointment threatens to overwhelm. But . . . God is with us!

If I take the wings of the morning and dwell in the uttermost parts of the sea, even there your hand shall lead me, and your right hand shall hold me.

Psalm 139:9–10

Even in the darkest times our Savior guards and strengthens us. He works in every detail of our lives for our good. He is with us. Always!

 PRAYER STARTER: Remind me, Lord, of your power and light, especially . . .

Protected from the Enemy

O my God; protect me from those who rise up against me.

Psalm 59:1

Natalie abruptly pushed herself away from the breakroom table and scrunched her lunch sack into a tight wad. Getting up, she tossed her trash into the basket. "Co-workers should be back soon," Natalie said to herself. She sighed as she contemplated the thought.

Her new job had seemed like a dream come true—at first. But then her co-workers began to shut her out of their conversations. More and more often they laughed at their private jokes, but whenever Natalie tried to join in, the conversation stopped altogether.

And then there were the rumors. Shortly after she was hired, Natalie's team began to speculate about management. Gossip about her boss's personal life derailed the agenda in nearly every planning meeting. Natalie didn't know how to handle it, let alone stop it.

Have you ever felt like Natalie? Have you ever felt pulled away from what you knew was right because you wanted so badly to be a part of the group? Maybe you repeated a lie or passed a rumor on to others, just to fit in or feel like you were "in the know."

Gossip. Lies. Innuendos. Rumors. We know they are wrong. Sometimes though, like Natalie, we may feel under attack. We long for protection from temptation, even as we dream up excuses to justify joining in. In times like that, the Holy Spirit reminds us:

We do not wrestle against flesh and blood, but against the rulers, against the authorities, against the cosmic powers over this present darkness, against the spiritual forces of evil in the heavenly places.

Ephesians 6:12

Satan himself is our actual enemy. The human beings around us are not. When we are tempted, we can run for shelter in the shadow of Christ's cross, the cross where Jesus fought temptation and defeated sin for us. The cross where our Savior crushed Satan's power. Forever.

There at the cross, we stand perfectly protected. Our Savior fights for us, even as he works in us, transforming us more and more into his very own image. Tap into his power. Today!

 PRAYER STARTER: Lord, help me recognize the true enemy. Remind me to run to you for protection and strength. Especially I ask . . .

Protected and Perfect

If we walk in the light, as he is in the light, we have fellowship with one another, and the blood of Jesus his Son cleanses us from all sin.

1 John 1:7

Glancing at her phone calendar, Kim saw tomorrow. Sunday. Kim wouldn't be going to church. In fact, she hadn't gone to church in three years. Three years! Ever since she'd said those things to Sara, done those things that so hurt her friend. She couldn't risk running into Sara. So Kim wouldn't be going to church tomorrow.

Guilt. It whispered constantly in Kim's ear. "You are despicable! How can you live with yourself?" The continual shame was like white noise, always playing in the back of her head. At first, Kim tried to convince herself that she'd done nothing wrong. When that failed, she tried to make excuses for her behavior. Finally, accepting what she'd said and done, Kim tried her best to forget about it. Over and done. But the whisper of guilt persisted.

At one time or another, each of us has been burdened by guilt. What does God think about our guilt? One of the most comforting verses on the subject comes from Psalms:

I confessed all my sins to you and stopped trying to hide my guilt. I said to myself, "I will confess my rebellion to the LORD." And you forgave me! All my guilt is gone.

Psalm 32:5 NLT

All guilt. Gone. God has forgiven you—completely—because of what Jesus did for you on the cross! Your sin has been washed away. Your shame is gone.

The next time you hear the Accuser's voice whispering words of reproach, be ready. Be ready to answer by speaking the truths of God's Word. You are forgiven. Completely. You wear the robe of Jesus' own righteousness, the spotless robe that belongs to you through faith.

This truth gives us the courage to ask forgiveness from those we've hurt. If they forgive us, that's great! All heaven celebrates with us the joy of that restored relationship. But even if others refuse to forgive, this truth remains glorious and certain: God has forgiven us. We are free from guilt, free from shame, perfectly protected from fear.

PRAYER STARTER: Thank you, Lord Jesus, for all . . .

Protected and Worry-Free

I will rejoice and be glad in your steadfast love, because you have seen my affliction; you have known the distress of my soul.

Psalm 31:7

Maggie's mind played and replayed her worries in a never-ending loop. "The baby's got a fever. She's probably getting another cold!" "This cold weather is sure to make the roads icy!" "The ice machine in the refrigerator is broken. Another bill!" "Our credit card bills are sky high!" "What if the baby's fever goes higher?" On and on it goes. One worry looping into the next. Maggie even worries about worrying too much!

Maggie is wise to be concerned about her constant worry! Worry can negatively affect your physical and mental health in serious ways. Consider: migraine headaches, ulcers, high blood pressure, difficulty sleeping, respiratory problems, weakening of the immune system, and much more. The saying "I'm worried sick" unfortunately rings true.

Have you ever wondered what causes worry? Many times, it's fear. Maggie is afraid that her baby will get sick, that

her bills can't be paid, and more. Psychologists suggest listing your worries on paper and categorizing them as "things I can control" and "things I cannot control." The simple act of noting your cares on paper seems to help calm the habit of constant worry.

Worrying is not a new phenomenon. In fact, Jesus gently addresses worry in his Sermon on the Mount:

Therefore I tell you, do not be anxious about your life, what you will eat or what you will drink, nor about your body, what you will put on. Is not life more than food, and the body more than clothing? Look at the birds of the air: they neither sow nor reap nor gather into barns, and yet your heavenly Father feeds them. Are you not of more value than they?

Matthew 6:25–26

The apostle John writes:

There is no fear in love, but perfect love casts out fear.

1 John 4:18

God's perfect love for you evicts all fear from your heart. In love, Jesus died for you. Your heavenly Father is strong to save! Next time you are worried, pray Scripture aloud. You might want to start with Joshua 1:9; Isaiah 41:10; Luke 1:37; and Philippians 4:19.

PRAYER STARTER: My Father, my King, your love evicts fear from my heart. Today I ask . . .

Heart Protection

You keep track of all my sorrows. You have collected all my tears in your bottle. You have recorded each one in your book.

Psalm 56:8 NLT

Amy brushed a sudden, unexpected tear from her cheek. Driving home from book club, she thought back to her friend Emma's words. "The baby hasn't slept for the past five nights! My husband has to get up for work, so guess who's had overnight baby duty?" Emma looked disgusted as she continued, "I am so glad to get away from them both tonight! I've really needed a break!"

Another tear slid past Amy's chin. Amy and her husband had been trying for over a year to get pregnant. Three different doctors, two specialists, countless tests and procedures, and a brief hospital stay for a miscarriage pretty well summed up the past fourteen months of Amy's life. And still no results.

"I know she didn't really mean anything by it," Amy whispered to herself as she stopped for a red light. "But,

I'd give just about anything to be able to stay awake all night, caring for a baby of my own." When the light turned green, Amy pulled the car to the curb and allowed herself to cry.

We all have our tender spots—areas in our lives that make us sensitive to the words and actions of others. In the clear light of day, we know that others didn't mean their words the way we initially interpreted them. Still, we hurt. Tears flow over lost dreams, fizzled plans, and unexpected misfortune.

Disappointment can make us feel isolated. Alone. We cry out, "No one knows what I'm going through!" But that's not true! God knows. He knows you personally, intimately. Not only does God know what you're going through, he's going through it with you. He sees every one of your setbacks and counts every one of your tears. He's your Father—a perfectly protective Father.

The eternal God is your dwelling place, and underneath are the everlasting arms.

Deuteronomy 33:27

When disappointment threatens to overwhelm you, run to your heavenly Father. Pour out your heart, and let him gently wipe away your tears. Sink into his strong arms. Be strengthened by his love.

 PRAYER STARTER: Lord Jesus, many emotions are stirring in my heart . . .

Since we belong to the day, let us be sober, having put on the breastplate of faith and love, and for a helmet the hope of salvation.

1 Thessalonians 5:8

Stumbling about in a dark room, fumbling for the light switch—we've all been there. What a relief when we find the switch and the light comes on. Suddenly, it's as if all darkness has vanished. Light streams into even the darkest corners, chasing shadows away.

Sometimes we forget that we belong to the Light— the Light of the world, Jesus! We forget that he's promised to perfectly protect us. Take a moment and memorize 1 Thessalonians 5:8. Ask that the Lord keep you from stumbling around in the darkness again!

Continually Kept

Peace I leave with you; my peace I give to you. Not as the world gives do I give to you. Let not your hearts be troubled, neither let them be afraid.

John 14:27

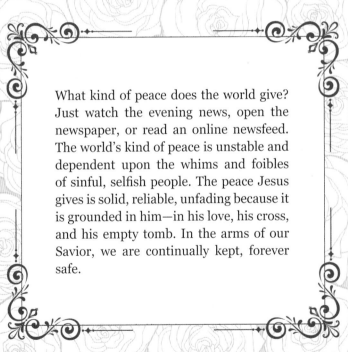

What kind of peace does the world give? Just watch the evening news, open the newspaper, or read an online newsfeed. The world's kind of peace is unstable and dependent upon the whims and foibles of sinful, selfish people. The peace Jesus gives is solid, reliable, unfading because it is grounded in him—in his love, his cross, and his empty tomb. In the arms of our Savior, we are continually kept, forever safe.

Kept in Heaven

Blessed be the God and Father of our Lord Jesus Christ! According to his great mercy, he has caused us to be born again to a living hope through the resurrection of Jesus Christ from the dead, to an inheritance that is imperishable, undefiled, and unfading, kept in heaven for you.

1 Peter 1:3–4

Jackie returns home from work to discover that Max, her dog, has ripped apart three decorative sofa pillows. Jackie sighs. The pillows are beyond repair.

Leah spends an afternoon rearranging the living room, only to find that she needs to put everything back, just the way it originally had been. Why? The sun shining through the windows had faded half of the sofa.

Carol frowns as she tosses away the block of cheese. "I needed this for tonight's dinner," she moaned. "But it looks like a third grader's science experiment!"

Diana sucks in her breath in an effort to help the zipper fasten more easily. "This dress fit perfectly last year," she mutters. Finally giving up, she sighs, "It's no use. I guess it's time for me to go shopping."

These four examples explain why we can't have nice things: bad stuff happens. Fabrics fade or shrink. Everything we count on eventually spoils or breaks. We may not even notice this process as it is happening, but change and decay occur anyway. Nothing we treasure here on earth will escape.

That's why our Lord keeps the very best, the very nicest of nice things, in the safest of all possible places—a place that sees no corruption. Ever. This best, most important treasure is your inheritance. It includes everything Jesus earned for you on Calvary's cross. And your Savior is keeping it safe for you in heaven.

Everything of true value is waiting there for you—all the beauty, the glory, the freedom of our heavenly home. No thief will break in there to steal it. You will never outgrow its blessings. That inheritance will keep its value forever.

You share in Jesus' resurrection right now. You have forgiveness and eternal life today! One day—sooner than you think—you will enjoy heaven, too. Christ himself is keeping it safe.

 PRAYER STARTER: Thank you, Lord Jesus, that my inheritance is secure! I pray for those who do not know you . . . .

Safe at Home

He who dwells in the shelter of the Most High will abide in the shadow of the Almighty. I will say to the LORD, "My refuge and my fortress, my God, in whom I trust."

Psalm 91:1–2

Picture your "dream home." Do you see a mansion, surrounded by lush landscaping? Do you imagine a four-car garage and grand front entrance? Step inside. Do you picture soaring ceilings, winding staircases, and walls of windows? Is the kitchen the size of your favorite restaurant? Are there more bathrooms than bedrooms? Can you get lost in the master bedroom closet? What a dream!

Or not. Perhaps your dream home looks nothing like the McMansion I just described. Maybe you're picturing something smaller—a tiny house! Small, but cozy at 175 square feet. See the little deck leading to the front door? Perfect for enjoying morning coffee. Just inside the door, two hooks beg to hold your coat or sweatshirt (and a friend's). See the cute little living room? It easily converts to a bedroom as you open the sofa. Imagine the miniature kitchen appliances and the way the table smartly folds flat against the wall when you're not eating. What a dream!

Ginormous, miniscule, or in between, no home is perfect unless it is safe. Remember the realtors' motto? Location. Location. Location. No matter the size, you want your home located in a safe location, a secure location.

The good news is that your perfect home does exist. Its location, though, may surprise you. Psalm 91:1–2 describes that location. Our Lord himself is the perfect dwelling place, the perfect refuge and fortress. Jesus describes it this way:

Whoever abides in me and I in him, he it is that bears much fruit, for apart from me you can do nothing.

John 15:5

As you go about your day—eating, working, relaxing—you abide in him, at peace, secure in his love, and sharing that love. Jesus made the shelter of the Most High your own when he suffered, died, and rose again for you. Welcome home!

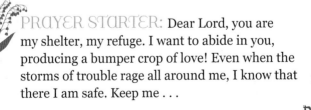

PRAYER STARTER: Dear Lord, you are my shelter, my refuge. I want to abide in you, producing a bumper crop of love! Even when the storms of trouble rage all around me, I know that there I am safe. Keep me . . .

Preciously Preserved

You have granted me life and steadfast love, and your care has preserved my spirit.

Job 10:12

The first people to settle the Wild West were hardy, resourceful folks. Pioneers knew how to hunt, trap, and fish for food. They knew how to plant gardens—one in the early spring and another in late summer—so that they could eat fresh vegetables and fruit for as many months as possible.

Early pioneers knew how to preserve food, too. They salted or smoked their meat. They used drying techniques or a pickling process to preserve many of their vegetables and fruits. Some of these preservation processes changed the taste of the original food—many times for the better!

Preservation continues to be important today. And not just in the kitchen or pantry! Job 10:12 reminds us that God is preserving something much more precious to him—it's you! Your heavenly Father loves you with an intense, fierce, passionate love. He intends to keep you close to himself at all costs. That's why Jesus, his Son, had to die. It's why God raised Jesus from the dead—so that you, too, could one day rise from your own death—to eternal life with him and his forever family in heaven.

What will the resurrected you be like? Here's a hint:

May the God of peace himself sanctify you completely, and may your whole spirit and soul and body be kept blameless at the coming of our Lord Jesus Christ. He who calls you is faithful; he will surely do it.

1 Thessalonians 5:23–24

"Your whole spirit and soul and body"—that's the real you. You will recognize your resurrected self! You will not become something or someone different. Rather, you will be the uniquely you God originally created you to be—but finally free from sin.

Just think about it: Your thoughts and emotions will be absolutely pure—completely free from selfishness. Your soul will enjoy absolute peace—no more turmoil or worry. Your body will be 100 percent healthy, robust. You will be able to wholly love God and others without the hindrance of sin or self-focus.

It's no wonder we pray: Come, Lord Jesus!

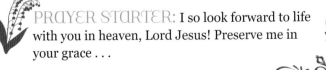

PRAYER STARTER: I so look forward to life with you in heaven, Lord Jesus! Preserve me in your grace . . .

No Collection Record

*If you, O LORD, should mark iniquities, O Lord,
who could stand?*

Psalm 130:3

Have you ever collected anything? Very young children often collect stuffed animals. Young adults may collect video games and CDs. Some adults get enjoyment from collecting stamps, coins, and artwork.

Serious collectors keep detailed records of the items within their collection. Extensive notes record the date, location, and price paid for each item. These records often help people relive their excitement about the special items within their collection.

Unfortunately, people often collect something else—a record of the wrongs by which others have hurt them. Here's how it happens:

- Someone on our morning commute abruptly cuts in front of us. We frown in fury as we lean on the car horn. We keep a record, remembering the incident so clearly that we recount the details of our exasperation with co-workers hours later at lunch and maybe more hours later with family members over dinner.

- When hurt by a friend or family member, we mentally record the incident. We add additional hurts to our collection day by day, week by week. We are all too eager to "share" our collection, many times without prompting, damaging everyone's relationships.

Our heavenly Father is not at all like this. He does not keep a record of our wrongs, collecting the details by which we have offended him. Instead, he transferred all of our sinful actions, harsh words, and hateful thoughts onto Jesus, our Savior, at Calvary's cross. Standing in the shadow of his cross, our burden is lifted. Our sins are gone. Completely! In exchange, we have a totally new lifestyle:

Put on then, as God's chosen ones, holy and beloved, compassionate hearts, kindness, humility, meekness, and patience, bearing with one another and, if one has a complaint against another, forgiving each other; as the Lord has forgiven you.

Colossians 3:12–13

Forgiveness never justifies another person's sin. It doesn't undo what happened in our past. But it does set in motion a much better future for us. Forgiving others frees us to live in peace and joy!

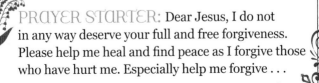

PRAYER STARTER: Dear Jesus, I do not in any way deserve your full and free forgiveness. Please help me heal and find peace as I forgive those who have hurt me. Especially help me forgive . . .

47

Simply Kept

*The LORD preserves the simple; when I was
brought low, he saved me.*

Psalm 116:6

"What do you want to be when you grow up?" It's a
question adults have asked children for generations.
The assumption made by most adults is that as children
grow older, they will mature. As they mature, children
will acquire more and more knowledge, perhaps making
them eligible for the job of their dreams. We encourage
children of all ages to "grow up" because we think that is
what's best for them.

When it comes to matters of faith, though, "Grow up!" is
not the Lord's admonition to his children. In fact, Jesus
advises just the opposite:

*I tell you the truth, unless you turn from your sins and
become like little children, you will never get into the
Kingdom of Heaven.*

Matthew 18:3 NLT

Jesus wasn't encouraging immature behavior. He wasn't
recommending that we remain forever dependent on
others. But he was encouraging a simple, childlike faith.
This kind of faith trusts the Father without reservation.
This kind of faith rests peacefully upon the One who
knows what's best for us and will bring good out of even
the worst of circumstances.

Too often we resent it when our plans are thwarted or interrupted, don't we? When calamity happens, we may shake our fist at God in anger and frustration. We act much like a small, sulky child, stamping her foot at not getting her own way.

In the cross of his Son, our heavenly Father forgives even these sins. He sends his Holy Spirit to work in us the faith he asks of us.

When we can't answer the whys or don't understand the ways of God, we can always trust his wisdom:

Trust in the LORD with all your heart, and do not lean on your own understanding.

Proverbs 3:5

When we attempt to figure out why God does the things he does or why he refuses to act when we think he should, his Holy Spirit calls us back to the basics: God loves you. Always and forever, you are his child.

 PRAYER STARTER: Father, help me trust in you. Especially now, I ask . . .

The LORD is your keeper.

Psalm 121:5

Psalm 121 was traditionally known as a traveling song. In times past, sojourners would sing this psalm as they set out on a journey.

Our lives are in many ways a journey. From birth to death, God keeps us always in his care. Even when troubles come, we are kept. When illness threatens, we are kept. No matter what happens, God is our keeper, and he ultimately will have the last word. That last word—the word God has for you—is this: You are mine forever!

Read Psalm 121. What is God saying to you in this psalm?

Enthusiastically Empowered

Awesome is God from his sanctuary; the God of Israel—he is the one who gives power and strength to his people. Blessed be God!

Psalm 68:35

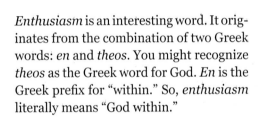

Enthusiasm is an interesting word. It originates from the combination of two Greek words: *en* and *theos*. You might recognize *theos* as the Greek word for God. *En* is the Greek prefix for "within." So, *enthusiasm* literally means "God within."

God is powerfully at work within your life right now. In the coming days, we'll discover what happens when we're enthusiastically empowered by our mighty and gracious Lord. Ready? Let's go!

Follow Enthusiastically

He calls his own sheep by name and leads them out. When he has brought out all his own, he goes before them, and the sheep follow him, for they know his voice.

John 10:3–4

What do cheerleaders do? Cheer, of course! They smile big and project their voices so that even spectators in the highest bleacher seats can hear and join in. Cheerleaders embody enthusiasm. Cheerleaders tumble and dance. They do whatever they can to get the fans excited, and they help the players get and keep a winning momentum.

Cheerleaders are important. They are indeed athletes, but they do not join the team. They stay on the sidelines, separated from the grueling and less glamorous effort that happens in the mud on the field.

When I read John 10:3–4, I am grateful that Jesus does so much more than cheer at us from the sidelines. Instead, our Savior leads. He's out ahead of us, calling us by name, urging us to follow. We'll never go anywhere Christ himself hasn't already been.

That's the miracle of God's plan of salvation. Jesus is our tested, victorious leader. Jesus knows what it's like to live in a sin-filled world. He's seen firsthand the hatred that originates in the hearts of sinful people. Jesus has experienced Satan's nagging temptations. Our Savior saw devastating illnesses with his own eyes. He watched as guilt over past sins ate away at desperate souls. Jesus has been there—down there in the muck and mud of life here on earth.

In addition, our Savior and Shepherd felt the horrible weight of sin—our sins. He suffered sin's ultimate penalty in our place. In great love for you and me, Jesus experienced death, eternal death—complete separation from his loving Father. But death did not—could not—hold our powerful Savior. Because of his victory, we enthusiastically follow Jesus—from death to life. Christ's resurrection guarantees it!

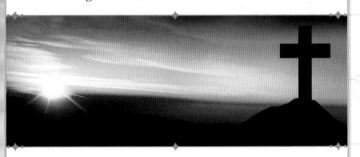

Even though I walk through the valley of the shadow of death, I will fear no evil, for you are with me.

Psalm 23:4

Jesus continues leading us today. No matter where we go, in sunshine or shadow, we walk in confidence and hope.

 PRAYER STARTER: Help me enthusiastically follow you, Lord Jesus, as you lead me today . . .

Power for Hope

But this I call to mind, and therefore I have hope:
The steadfast love of the LORD never ceases; his
mercies never come to an end; they are new every
morning; great is your faithfulness.

Lamentations 3:21–23

"I don't suppose anyone would want to go with me.
Nobody ever does." Eeyore, the donkey featured in
Winnie-the-Pooh books, has a gloomy outlook on life.
Describing his home, Eeyore comments in his slow, sad
drawl, "It's not much of a house, just right for not much of
a donkey." Eeyore sees his life through a dismal lens. Yet,
even young readers feel an endearing connection to the
forlorn little donkey. Maybe we all do . . .

Life has its moments—those unbelievably fantastic
moments—like scoring the winning goal, landing the job
of your dreams, marrying your soul mate. But (there had
to be a *but* coming, right?) many moments in our life are
not all that great. Your team loses to the worst team in
the league. You're downsized out of a job. You no longer
recognize your soul mate as you read his demands in the
divorce documents. Life is hard. Just ask Eeyore.

Scientists have learned that self-talk like Eeyore's is not
helpful. Does your self-talk tend toward the negative? If
so, it's not surprising. Our sinful selves are prone toward
it. Satan eggs us on in this direction. While Eeyore voices
his negative self-talk aloud, we may keep it to ourselves.
Either way, though, it is harmful to our spirit.

Your heavenly Father, your Creator, knew all about self-talk long before scientists named and studied it. Because he made you, and because your Father knows that his perfectly created world is now stained with sin, he sees your inclination to take a negative perspective. Your heavenly Father understands, but it's not what he wants for his dear children—you included. Not at all!

Instead, our Lord urges us to remember his past faithfulness—especially his faithfulness to forgive us in the cross of Christ. He continually calls us back to himself in repentance and faith. He reminds us that he is for us, always encouraging us to depend on him, day after day—today and always!

 PRAYER STARTER: Lord, remind me of your faithfulness today . . .

Serving with Enthusiasm

To each is given the manifestation of the Spirit for the common good.

1 Corinthians 12:7

"It's not here." Nine-year-old Amy flopped herself down on the family room sofa, disappointment etched on her face. "When will Aunt Lucy's present come?" she whined. "My birthday was a week ago! Mom, are you *sure* she sent a gift to me?"

It's hard to wait. Waiting for something we really want is especially hard. Sometimes Christians feel like Amy as we wait for our spiritual gift.

Search online to learn "How can I identify my spiritual gifts?" and you will receive over 700,000 answers. Dig a little deeper into the results, and you'll find countless tools, questionnaires, and assessments designed to help.

Sometimes a "gifts inventory" will open our minds to serving in ways we hadn't ever considered. Other times, though, we may be tempted to use the idea of a "spiritual gift" as a convenient excuse: "Oh, I can't help fold service bulletins. It's just not my spiritual gift." When we take attitudes like this, we may waste opportunities to serve simply because we haven't yet identified our gift.

The Holy Spirit does not want our spiritual gifts to remain a mystery. Rather than agonizing over questionnaires, you might instead simply begin to serve where God has placed you. Right here. Right now.

For instance, you might ask yourself, "What is my occupation? What have I been trained to do? What is my area of expertise?" Perhaps your answers will point you toward an area of service.

Or think about what you enjoy doing outside your workplace. Maybe God will use your hobby or personal interests to form new relationships and, through those relationships, open doors to larger service.

Finally, consider what other people have told you: "Wow! You're really good at *(fill in the blank)*." Could those comments be an indication of your spiritual giftedness? Of course!

If you're still not sure, contact your local church, food pantry, or homeless shelter and offer your assistance. Spend time in prayer, interceding for college students, young families, those in the military, and your pastor. Pray that they grow closer to Jesus and use their own spiritual gifts to his glory.

PRAYER STARTER: Lord, I want to use the gifts you have given me. Guide me today as I . . .

Enthusiastically Run

Let us run with endurance the race that is set before us, looking to Jesus, the founder and perfecter of our faith, who for the joy that was set before him endured the cross, despising the shame, and is seated at the right hand of the throne of God.

Hebrews 12:1–2

Diana Nyad swam—and swam and swam and swam! For almost 55 hours, the 64-year-old woman swam—all the way from Cuba to Key West, Florida. Nyad faced sharks, jellyfish, and dangerous man-of-wars on her journey through the Straits of Florida. Weakened by the exertion, she could barely speak as she stood at last on Florida's sandy beach.

What kept her going as she battled a fierce headwind for 49 hours and encountered countless lethal ocean creatures? Nyad says she endured because of the "team effort"—referring to the five support boats that accompanied her. "It looks like a solitary sport, but it's a team," Nyad told reporters.

Diana Nyad's story is inspirational, with some parallels to our lives as Christians. Like Nyad, we face daily challenges and often feel like giving up. Many of us enjoy a supportive "team"—fellow believers in Christ—who stay close to help us and offer encouragement.

Like Nyad, we also will endure but not because we are strong, not because we trained and mentally prepared, not because we are so good at living a godly life. No, it's nothing we've done or could even hope to accomplish. It's everything Jesus has done for us!

Take heart; I have overcome the world.

John 16:33

The work is done! The race is won! Jesus is victorious—overcoming sin, death, and Satan—all for us! Now our Savior joins us in our struggles, giving us his strength, pouring his own enduring power into us. What's more, his death guarantees our reward—a crown of righteousness in heaven.

Henceforth there is laid up for me the crown of righteousness, which the Lord, the righteous judge, will award to me on that day, and not only to me but also to all who have loved his appearing.

2 Timothy 4:8

 PRAYER STARTER: Lord, remind me of your victory. Enable me to anticipate with enthusiasm the crown of righteousness you have earned for me. Today especially . . .

Enthusiastically Equipped

*May the God of peace who brought again from
the dead our Lord Jesus, the great shepherd of the
sheep, by the blood of the eternal covenant, equip
you with everything good that you may do his will.*

Hebrews 13:20–21

Knee-high socks, shin guards, soft-cleat shoes, and a
black-and-white ball. What are these? The equipment
necessary for soccer.

Roasting pan, poultry lifters, roaster rack, meat baster,
thermometer, carving knife, and large platter. What are
these? The equipment necessary to roast a turkey.

Equipment is important no matter what you are
attempting to do. The right equipment can help you
quickly and successfully accomplish a task. So, what kind
of equipment do we need for doing God's will?

Primarily, the Word of God!

The Holy Spirit uses that Word to bring us to saving faith
in Jesus, our Savior. He uses the Scripture to correct and
teach us, to encourage, support, and strengthen us. Just
as proper equipment energizes sports teams for activity,
God's Word energizes us for work in his kingdom.

God uses his Word to soften our hearts and to create in
our hearts genuine concern and love for others. Properly
outfitted, we are ready to serve our Lord by serving the

people around us. We are ready to face what life brings, no matter what. Properly equipped by our Lord, we bring him glory in our words and actions.

You are precious to God and dearly loved by him. He wants you to know him more deeply, trust him more fully, and rely more consistently on his unquenchable love for you. He will work these things in you as you listen to him.

He speaks to you through his Word. Do you hear that Word proclaimed from the pulpit on Sunday morning? Listen to it! Do you read that Word on your own through the week? Pay attention to it! Do you have a friend in Christ who discusses that Word with you? Continue to cultivate that practice.

The Bible is God's love letter to you! Your Lord speaks to you through it. He wants you to know—really know for certain—that you belong to him. You are precious—so very precious, and dearly, dearly loved—eternally!

 PRAYER STARTER: Dear Lord, energize me through your Word, and equip me . . .

I will be your God throughout your lifetime—until your hair is white with age. I made you, and I will care for you. I will carry you along and save you.

Isaiah 46:4 NLT

Talk about enthusiastic encouragement—God not only formed us and knew us before we were born, he's promised to take care of us until we breathe our final breath on this earth! He will carry us when life's burdens weigh us down, and he will one day, at last, bring us into his nearer presence. There, we will understand his love for us in richer ways than we can even imagine right now.

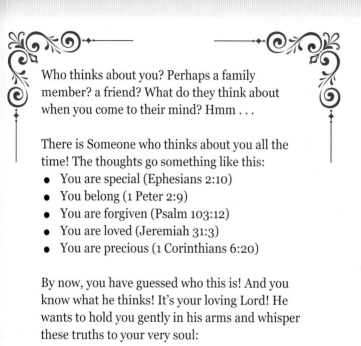

Who thinks about you? Perhaps a family member? a friend? What do they think about when you come to their mind? Hmm . . .

There is Someone who thinks about you all the time! The thoughts go something like this:

- You are special (Ephesians 2:10)
- You belong (1 Peter 2:9)
- You are forgiven (Psalm 103:12)
- You are loved (Jeremiah 31:3)
- You are precious (1 Corinthians 6:20)

By now, you have guessed who this is! And you know what he thinks! It's your loving Lord! He wants to hold you gently in his arms and whisper these truths to your very soul:

"I love you—dearly love you! You are precious—so precious—to me! You are mine—forever—mine!"

Lord God, hold me close. Today. Tomorrow. Forever. Amen.

To see all of CTA's devotion books and journals, visit us at www.CTAinc.com.

If this book has made a difference in your life or if you have simply enjoyed it, we would like to hear from you. Your words will encourage us!

E-mail: editor@CTAinc.com; include the subject line: PDL18SC

Write: Editorial Manager, Department PDL18SC CTA, Inc. PO Box 1205 Fenton, MO 63026-1205

Comment online: www.CTAinc.com (search PDL18SC)